Stories
from the
Caribbean

by
Petronella Breinburg

Illustrated by
Syrah Arnold and Tina Barber

RAINTREE
STECK-VAUGHN
P U B L I S H E R S
A Steck-Vaughn Company

Austin, Texas
www.steck-vaughn.com

OTHER MULTICULTURAL STORIES:

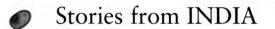

 Stories from THE AMAZON

Stories from CHINA

Stories from INDIA

Stories from NATIVE AMERICA

Stories from WEST AFRICA

Published by Raintree Steck-Vaughn Publishers,
an imprint of Steck-Vaughn Company

Library of Congress Cataloging-in-Publication Data
Breinburg, Petronella.
The Caribbean / Petronella Breinburg.
p.   cm.—(Multicultural stories)
Includes bibliographical references.
ISBN 0-7398-1334-X (hard)
0-7398-2032-X (soft)
1. Caribbean—Juvenile literature.
[1. Caribbean.]
I. Title. II. Series.

Printed in Italy. Bound in the United States.
1 2 3 4 5 6 7 8 9 0 04 03 02 01 00

Acknowledgments: Artwork on pages 11, 12, 18, 26, 27, 32, 36, and 43 is
by Tina Barber. All other artwork, including page borders, is by Syrah Arnold.

Contents

Introduction

As with so many children in the Caribbean, my lessons in school were about Europe. I lived in Surinam, a colony of a European country. We were taught about Holland, which governed us from afar, not about the country in which we lived.

How did we find out about our own places and our own people? Through our stories. The Caribbean is rich in stories and their tellers: men living at the mines, away from their families, amusing themselves with tales told at night; special stories for birthdays or coming-of-age ceremonies; stories of ghosts told on a cool evening as it starts to get dark.

Where did our stories come from? From all the peoples of the Caribbean: African slaves; European colonists and slave owners; Indian and Chinese laborers; even, maybe, the original peoples, the Arawaks and Caribs. Often, over the years, the stories from those different places blended together to become something new.

My aunt was a *Nenne Dofi*, a Great Storyteller. No one ever got tired of listening to her stories; sometimes when I was alone I pretended to be my aunt, telling a favorite tale. As soon as I was old enough I began to travel across the Caribbean, collecting stories for myself. This book contains a few of my favorites, which I hope you will like as much as I do. The first is the story of a Dupie, from Jamaica. . .

Petronella Breinburg

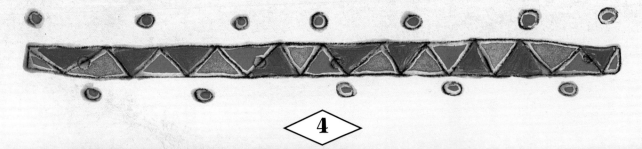

UNITED STATES

BAHAMAS

The Caribbean's place in the world

ATLANTIC OCEAN

CUBA

DOMINICAN REPUBLIC

HAITI

PUERTO RICO

LEEWARD ISLANDS

JAMAICA

WINDWARD ISLANDS

CARIBBEAN SEA

NETHERLANDS ANTILLES

ARUBA

BONAIRE
CURAÇAO

TOBAGO

TRINIDAD

VENEZUELA

GUYANA

SURINAM

FRENCH GUIANA

THE CARIBBEAN

Northern parts of Venezuela, Guyana, Surinam, and French Guiana are culturally part of the Caribbean, even though geographically they are part of South America. They share a history of colonization and slavery that makes them more like the Caribbean than South America. Today there are still close links between them, as you can see from the last story in the book, Papa Bois.

HAUNTING TALES

On one of my story-finding trips to Jamaica I was mesmerized by stories about hauntings, which are very common there. I was also told that there were Bre-nancy stories brought from Africa, and many other varieties of stories in Jamaica. These different stories came from the many racial backgrounds of the Jamaican people: from the African, Asian, and European continents. But the haunting stories were always the ones I liked best; often these ghostly tales reflect the history of the place in which they're told.

The spirits of dead people who wander around at night are called Dupies. I had listened to many types of stories, but the Dupie story that fascinated me the most is the one that I listened to late one night, as the darkness seemed to close in. The tale of how Sunny-Limp walked again . . .

ATLANTIC OCEAN

JAMAICA

CARIBBEAN SEA

Sunny-Limp Walks Again

"You asked," said the storyteller, Shorty Brown, looking serious. "I'll tell you, the young lord murdered his wife. He did murder her on this very estate. He was helped in that foul deed by his man Sunny-Limp. They murdered her, the poor pretty woman. They murdered her on this very same day some hundred years ago, 1882 to the day. And she was not even guilty as charged. No wonder they haunt this place.

"Many young girls who live here have seen her. Some heard her wails. Some heard Sunny-Limp's wooden leg thumping, thump, thump. . ." Shorty Brown stopped talking. He was waiting for the drink he knew was to come.

Shorty Brown was a caretaker at a girls' boarding school, but he also told stories to tourists or whoever wanted to listen.

Louise listened but tried not to laugh. She didn't believe in all this ghost nonsense. Louise had come to stay with her aunt and cousin for the school holidays. Her aunt lived on a large school compound where she was in charge. In the old days, that large compound had been part of a sugar plantation full of black slaves.

One of the older people handed Shorty Brown a bottle. Shorty Brown took several mouthfuls and with a "Brr. . . goooooood. . . brrrr," shook his head. Then he continued the story of murder and hauntings and Dupies, who Louise learned were ghosts.

Shorty Brown drank some more from the bottle. The more he drank, Louise noticed, the spookier the story became. Shorty Brown put on a creepy voice: "Lord Mains stalks the castle searching for his unfaithful wife. He discovers her trembling form at the foot of the spiral staircase. The door to the dungeons is locked. She can flee no further. She cries for mercy: 'Please, don't do it!'

"'You unfaithful wench!' cries Lord Mains, clutching her throat. His hands are so strong they could kill a bear. Her limp form falls against him. He throws her aside like a rag doll and unlocks the door into the dungeon, that to this day is a secret passage."

The story was getting more bizarre and spooky the more Shorty Brown drank, so Louise's aunt said that it was very late and the girls should go to bed. They had to be ready for the early morning trip up the Blue Mountain.

Louise's room was in the girls' corridor, next door to Chrissy's. Chrissy was yawning so much that Louise thought she had better not go in.

"I'll wake up in the morning," said Chrissy by the door. She was still yawning!

"Remember that we leave at 5 o'clock in the morning, not in the afternoon." Louise laughed.

In her room, Louise sat by her window to admire the beautiful sky and the high blue mountains nearby. A bullfrog croaked and Louise became worried that the creature might be in her room. She quickly looked around. There was no frog to be seen, yet the croaking sounded as if it was in the room. Outside, the wind began to make loud, peculiar noises.

The sound became so loud that Louise got worried and thought that she had better get Chrissy. Her cousin would be used to these frogs and, after all, it's better to be scared with a friend than on your own. Still in her day dress, Louise crept on tiptoe so as not to disturb anyone other than Chrissy. (Also, if that *was* a huge frog and it heard her, it might jump on her.)

Louise turned left. She remembered Chrissy's room was to the left of her room. Was that right? She wasn't sure now, and the passage looked dark and spooky.

Someone snored, but who? Young
girls don't snore. Only old people snore.
Louise went to knock at a door but changed her mind.
What if it was one of the other girls' rooms and not
Chrissy's? Ah, the telephone—she could call her aunt.
There. . . Where?. . . Where?. . . There was a telephone just
by the staircase, remembered Louise.

Thump! Thump! THUMP! went a startling noise. At first
it was faint but then it got louder. Louise almost jumped out
of her skin, she was so scared. She began to walk faster for
the telephone.

Thump! Thump! THUMP!

"Who's there?" she called out.

No answer, just THUMP! THUMP! THUMP! as if
someone was banging a walking stick on the floor. Louise
began to run, but the thumping got louder behind her.

She must get out, but which door? Where was the key to open the gate, to get out on the lawn?

Louise felt a clamminess that seemed to be pressing in on her. She felt a peculiar chill, even though earlier it had been a warm night.

Louise looked at her watch. It was five minutes to midnight. "The hour the ghost walks," Shorty Brown had said. "Don't be stupid," she said. "Don't think of nonsense like that! Calm down! Think, think what to do."

She found the phone. Quickly, she picked up the receiver. She looked at her watch again—four minutes to midnight. Suddenly, the single bulb in the vaulted ceiling started to flicker. "Oh, no! Don't go out—please, God, don't let the light go out!" Phone. . . phone. . . If only the light held out.

Suddenly it went dark. Louise's grip on the receiver tightened with fear. The blackness now surrounding her was so deep she could feel it, but still she didn't panic: she could dial in the dark.

Then something cold and clammy found the back of her neck. Louise screamed. She screamed loud. She screamed long! Still screaming, Louise turned and, with the telephone receiver, beat at whatever it was that had touched her neck. Flinging down the receiver, she threw herself against the stone wall, except that it wasn't stone. She felt wood, a door! It must be a door, or was it the floor? "So, I have found you at last," said a slow, grating voice, that didn't belong to Shorty Brown. Louise became aware of a strange light in front of her. The kilted figure of Lord Mains was descending the stairs toward her, hands outstretched; hands strong enough to kill a bear! The voice rose to a terrible roar: "You unfaithful wench!"

Louise opened her mouth, but no scream came. Her limp form fell against the figure of Lord Mains.

He threw her aside like a rag doll and unlocked the door to the dungeons. The grip around her throat had nearly stifled her, yet Louise kept screaming. . .

Someone rubbed her palm and called "Louisa!" It was her aunt's pet name for her, "Louisa." Louise opened her eyes to see several people staring at her.

"What you doing down here, and how did you get here?" asked her cousin, Chrissy.

"Yes, why down here?" asked someone else, "why down here?"

"It was Sunny-Limp. He brought her for Lord Mains. She soon turn young lady, so he brought her."

"Don't talk stupid, Shorty Brown. You're scaring the girls," said Louise's aunt. "No such thing as a kilted ghost called Lord Mains."

Louise did not agree. But, somehow, she thought it best not to say so.

STORIES FOR BRE-NANCY

Before my arrival in Guyana, I had heard a great deal about Guyana Jumbies, which were the spirits of dead people. In particular, I had heard about the Dutch Jumbies: the white spirits of the Dutch who ruled Guyana for many years. Then, when the British were about to take over, the Dutch hid the gold they had dug out of Guyana's mines. There were many stories, some of them gory, about what people did for the Dutch Jumbies so they could find out where the gold was hidden.

During my years in Guyana, I heard a variety of stories from the multicultural population. I liked the Jumbie stories, but preferred one of the more serious stories about Bre-nancy and the 13 Plantains. Bre-nancy is a character from West Africa, who arrived in Guyana during the days of slavery.

ATLANTIC OCEAN

JAMAICA

CARIBBEAN SEA

GUYANA

The story that follows comes from Guyana, but Bre-nancy is a popular character across the Caribbean, especially in Jamaica.

Bre-nancy
and the
13 plantains

It was a cool evening and getting dark in Guyana. The children of Pleasance, by the coast, came out to play. They were roasting crabs, sweet potatoes, and plantains on an open fire. The local old man came to sit, as he usually did, to eat with the children. The old man, whose name no one knew, held a plantain in his hand, and the children knew at once that there would be a story, and that it would be one to do with plantains. The old man always told them stories about things he held in his hand or was pointing to.

"This one," began the old man, and the children gathered to sit around him. "This one is a plantain story or a story about how Bre-nancy, himself a trickster, got tricked. Now Bre-nancy, who we all know, is a man who turns himself into a huge spider. Well, Bre-nancy always depended on his brain to get by, but his brain and his cunning often failed him.

"One day Bre-nancy needed
food, not only for himself, but also for
his wife and their twelve children.

"His wife had just chased him out of the
house with a broom and told him not to return
until he found food. Bre-nancy did not want to stay
out of his own home, but neither did he want to get his
hands dirty or get sweat pouring down his face: 'Not fair,
not fair,' he muttered while walking up and down the road
with his hands behind his back. 'Not fair, got to find food
for thirteen people and myself. How, eh, how?'

"But no matter how hard Bre-nancy tried, no idea came.
That is, not until he heard someone groaning in the
distance. He went to peer behind the bushes and saw that
it was Bre-bush Rat. 'Ah, good day to you, my good
neighbor,' said Bre-nancy.

"'Hi, Bre-nancy,' said Bre-bush Rat, trying to hide a
bunch of plantains. 'How are your wife and children?'

"'Where did you get all those plantains from?' asked Bre-nancy, already planning to cheat Bre-bush Rat.

"'I worked on a farm and this is my whole week's pay.'

"'That's nice.' said Bre-nancy, craftily.

"'Of course it is!' shouted Bre-bush Rat. 'You leave my plantains alone.'

"'Come on, my friend. . . .' Bre-nancy gave Bre-bush Rat a very friendly smile. 'I'll help carry it, and you give me some for my family, eh? I don't want any for myself, only for the wife and children, I swear.'

"'OK, then.' Bre-bush Rat gave Bre-nancy exactly thirteen plantains, one for each of his children and one for his wife.

"Bre-nancy got home and watched his wife roast the plantains and give one to each of his children and keep one for herself. He sat down and made his face look as sad as possible.

"'Oh,' said Ma-nancy, 'you take mine.' And she pushed her plantain in front of Bre-nancy.

"'No, no,' he said.

"'You have half of mine,' said the first child and at once broke the plantain in half.

"'And half of mine,' said the second, then the third and then the fourth. Soon each child had given half of his or her plantain to their dad. Each time Bre-nancy at first refused but then took it and ate it all up.

Ma-nancy had an idea.

"'Tell me, good husband, how many half plantains have you eaten and how many whole plantains that makes?'

"'Oh, eh, eh. . . .' Poor Bre-nancy. He could not say. He got out and began to walk up and down with two of his legs behind his back. And he still is walking now, trying to figure out how many plantains he had."

The old man laughed and took another roasted plantain. The children laughed, too. Even the little ones knew what Bre-nancy did not.

STORIES FROM THE NETHERLANDS ANTILLES

As children in Surinam we learned a great deal about the Netherlands Antilles. These islands are many miles apart but they all have something in common. Their stories often had a Carib or Arawak origin and were dramatized by the storyteller. St. Maarten stories are mainly about mountain spirits and nature, explaining things like day and night and hurricanes. I heard Curaçao tales from one of my cousins who lived there.

My favorite, as a teenager, was the one about two strange crows. In St. Maarten some people think that crows flying past a wedding bring good luck and happiness, because the crows were really Toewi and Kroemoe. Of course, I didn't believe, but just for good measure, when I was a bridesmaid for the first time, I kept looking up at the sky. . .

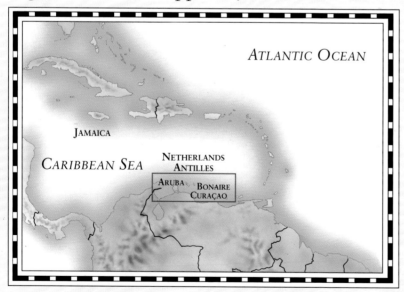

ATLANTIC OCEAN

JAMAICA

CARIBBEAN SEA

NETHERLANDS ANTILLES

ARUBA BONAIRE CURAÇAO

Toewi and Kroemoe

Lilieth's sister is getting married and Lilieth is to be a bridesmaid. One of her duties is to keep looking up into the sky now and again. She must look for two strange crows flying past. If they fly past, it will be a lucky marriage. The crows were once Toewi and Kroemoe—their story goes back many years.

There are many versions of the story about Toewi and Kroemoe, but they all start the same way. . . .

At that time, there lived a beautiful girl called Toewi. Some versions of her story say that she was one of the Arawak tribe. Other storytellers are sure that she was one of the Caiquetio tribe, which was different from the Arawaks because Caiquetio girls were even more beautiful. Toewi had golden brown skin and long black braids that hung down her back. Toewi liked to sing and she sang beautifully. When she sang, many birds came to listen to her song. Even the crows came to listen to her, though they stayed at a distance so that no one would throw stones at them.

Toewi liked to imagine things. She often
pretended to herself that she had flown away into
the sky to be a young princess, married to the sky
prince. Then she would sing and dance around. Toewi
also had to do chores; she had to carry water from the
river and to help with the weaving of cotton into cloth.
But she didn't mind the chores. She sang happily while
carrying water on her shoulder or while weaving.

One day Toewi was weaving and singing as usual.
There were birds, even crows, listening from outside.
So busy was Toewi with weaving, humming, and
pretending that it was a long time before she
noticed that a young man had come to
stand by the doorway.

"Oh, my parents are away and you can't come in."

The young man, dressed in all the finery of a young warrior, just smiled. If, thought Toewi, he was a young warrior, then he could not be a rain god because a rain god did not fight, and the rain god was old, very old, with a very long beard. Aloud, she said, "My people are away. You must come back when they return." Toewi stared; for a while she could not speak. The young warrior might well be a chief's son, judging from his headdress. In any case, she should not be talking to him, and she had to tell him to go away. "Come back when my father is at home." So the stranger left.

On the next day, Toewi had to bring water from the river. She was singing again that day, when suddenly the same young warrior appeared in front of her.

Again, the young warrior did not speak. He just stood there and smiled. Toewi spoke first. She had completely forgotten that she was not to talk to strangers and said, "I am not seeing you. You're in my pretend game. You don't really exist. That's it, you're in my pretending game."

The young man did not reply. He simply stepped forward and helped Toewi put the earthen jug on her head. She remembered that this young warrior was only a person in her pretend game. The young warrior followed Toewi until she got home.

26

After that day, Toewi eagerly went to the river to get water. Sometimes, she went to get water even when the family did not really need water. Every day, the handsome young warrior appeared, but never said a word. Every day, the birds sat in the distance and listened to her singing. The crows, too, listened. The young warrior in all his finery would also sit at a distance and listen to Toewi's singing.

One day while Toewi sang, a flock of crows came very near, and some flew close to her head. No one liked crows in the village. Toewi picked up a stone and threw it at the flock.

"Stupid crows." She laughed and then threw another stone, this time a larger one.

"Stop! Don't do that!" shouted the young warrior. "Do you know what you have done?"

Suddenly, before Toewi's
eyes, the young warrior turned
into a large and strange-looking crow—Kroemoe,
the King of the Crows. Before Toewi could stop him, he
grabbed her by her long braid and flew away with her.

Just at that moment some young children were coming to
fetch water and saw it all. The children shouted and began
to throw sticks and stones, even handfuls of sand, but the
more they chased and threw things, the higher the crow
took Toewi. Toewi shouted to the ground, "Don't throw
things; you'll kill us. Don't kill us!"

Toewi was never seen again.

One very old villager told the people that Toewi had been
turned into a crow by Kroemoe. Now she is the Queen of
the Crows and is happy.

Lilieth, who was to be a bridesmaid, had waited for a
long time. Then, suddenly, the crows came. Two strange but
beautiful crows flapped their wings and flew past, very low
indeed!

Anana, the Maker

This is a story from St. Maarten

"**S**hhh. . ." said Theo. Theo's great grandmother leaned forward, and Theo's friends who had come to play began to listen.

Theo's great grandmother had come to England from all the way across the Atlantic Ocean, where she lived. She had come to visit from Surinam, at the edge of the Caribbean. Great grandmother told good stories. Sometimes the stories were funny and sometimes they were sad.

"It is so dark tonight," said Theo's great grandmother.

"What do they call a dark night with no moon showing, Avo?" asked Theo, using the name he was told meant great grandmother.

"Mmm. . . well, there are tales about dark nights and about two brothers. One brother was called Moon, the other was called Sun. But the two brothers were both very different. Sun was thinking of only good things, but Moon was thinking of nothing but evil. These two brothers always fought each other. So the Maker, or Anana, as the slaves called the creator of the world, had to find a way to keep them apart. One day Anana waved his golden wings and said to both brothers, 'You may each have half of every day, so that you will not squabble any more. Go and let me see what each of you can create.'"

"Anana told each brother to make what he wanted for his half of every day.

"At first, Moon created evil beasts. Soon, however, he was not satisfied with just his beasts, so he created evil in hurricanes, rain storms, and very dark nights. He created evil in trees, poisonous flowers, everything he could think of. If it had not been for Sun's goodness, the Earth would have been full of Moon's evil creations. But Sun stepped in.

"Sun created good animals, which Moon could not turn evil no matter how hard he tried. Sun created some good in man that Moon, no matter how hard he tried, could not turn evil. Moon thought that if he were not careful, he would have no evil creations left. Moon got his strongest, most evil creations together and told them, 'We must get rid of the Sun.'

"Moon got an evil jaguar to try and swallow the Sun. Sun was no weakling. Sun always managed to escape from the grip of his enemies. He also had the power to burn those who ran after him. The first time Sun used that power was when the worst of Moon's evil creations tried to swallow him up. Moon was really vexed when he saw that Sun had managed to escape from the grip of the worst, the fiercest, of his creations, the Moon Jaguar. In fact, Moon was so vexed, he created more and more of these evil Moon Jaguars.

"Because Sun had turned out to be so hard to beat, Moon tried to trick him. Moon disappeared at the time he should have left the earth because it was Sun's turn. But Moon would leave some of his evil creations behind. Moon even got some clouds to work with him. He got them to run after Sun and grab him before Sun had a chance to wake up properly. But Sun burned the clouds away.

"Moon got some of his worst beasts, some of them very fierce indeed with huge colored spots on their bodies, to join in the attack against Sun. Moon sent those evil and fierce beasts to catch Sun. Each time, Moon would create more and more evil and fierce beasts to run after Sun, trying to swallow him up completely.

"Occasionally, a beast would succeed, but each time Sun would struggle and finally burn his way out of the grip of his evil brother's creation.

"Today," uttered Theo's great grandmother, "we call that the eclipse, but the Amerindians believed that it was Moon's evil creation, the Moon Jaguar, swallowing up the Sun. When the eclipse ended, it meant Sun had escaped again."

"Dinner time," called Theo's mother.

"Cakes!" shouted Theo's friends.

SLAVE STORIES FROM SURINAM

I grew up in Beekhuize, which was once a huge Dutch family plantation. A canal divided the town. The canal linked two rivers, one on each side, to form a huge "H" shape.

The Maroons, whom the Dutch called *Bosch Negers*, or Bush Negroes, traveled along the Saramaka River into Beekhuize. These Maroons were the descendants of slaves who had escaped to live in the rain forest. On the other side of the "H" shape was the Surinam River: all along the river tales about runaway slaves were still told. My favorite was the story of the Flying Slaves, perhaps because it was dramatized for me at my own "rite-of-passage" ceremony. I hope you like it.

ATLANTIC OCEAN

LEEWARD ISLANDS

WINDWARD ISLANDS

CARIBBEAN SEA

SURINAM

The Flying Slaves

Stefan was very proud, and his friends also looked at him with pride. The storyteller, who some Surinamese people call a Greo, had arrived. In fact, Stefan was as proud as a peacock in his grandmother's yard. His pride came from being the younger brother of the girl whose special ceremony was taking place. The ceremony was because his sister was over ten years old now, and no longer a little girl.

Then Stefan watched his sister come in; she was dressed in an African panji because they were pretending that she was an African princess. Stefan liked the ceremony; he liked the food even though it was cooked without salt. But what Stefan liked best of all was the storytelling. He liked the way the Greo dressed up and waved magic anjisas around when she spoke.

"Sit here," said Stefan, showing his friends and his sister's friends where to sit.

"Er tin tin," began the storyteller.

"Anansy mek tin," replied all the children.

Stefan had no idea what that saying meant. He knew, though, that you always said it before a storyteller begins.

"Kri" called the storyteller and waved her magic anjisa.

"Kra!" shouted all the children. "Anansy brok em back!"

"Many, many, many years ago, your ancestors and mine were brought from Africa in chains, in heavy chains, digging into their flesh!

"Once here, the Africans were treated very badly. They were beaten; they were sold on a market stand just the same as we sell chickens and goats in the market today. Children often screamed as their mothers were sold and taken away elsewhere, never to be seen again. Mothers screamed as their children were taken away." The storyteller paused to wave two anjisas before continuing.

"Many slaves escaped to live in the bush," the storyteller continued, "but one group that had not escaped heard that if they did not eat salt, they would be able to fly back to Africa. Desperate people believe anything and these people were desperate, so that group stopped eating salt. However, the children of the slaves worked in the white people's houses. They had to eat whatever the masters and their children had left, and that food had salt in it.

"If their mothers and fathers who worked in the fields did not eat salt, they would soon be flying away, leaving the children behind. The children had an idea. They secretly began to put tiny amounts of salt in their parents' food.

"The day of the flight came. There was a big ceremony; people dressed up in their best panji. The drums roared and sent messages across the land. A group of five slaves who were to be the first to fly back to Africa held hands and walked up Mabo Hill, which still stands today. The five were followed by every slave from across the Para area.

"The five slaves, still holding hands, jumped.

"The five did not fly; their bodies could not fly away. Their bodies were later found at the bottom of Mabo Hill. Some people said that the spirits of the five did fly away, back home to Africa.

"But one thing that everyone knows is that Surinam Kreoroes put very little salt in their food and ceremonial food never has salt in it."

Stefan watched as the storyteller went to the ceremonial stool where his sister sat. He heard the storyteller say: "Rise and fly away, daughter. Fly away to your fortune, even without wings!" The storyteller got up, waved her anjisas, and then silently left.

Stefan did not understand any of this. All he knew was that those ceremonies were great fun and he enjoyed the storytelling.

TRINIDAD & SURINAM

When I was a schoolgirl, visits between Surinam and Trinidad were very common. Each had a large Asian population with its own Hindu folklore, alongside an African population with its own folklore. Often, there were heated arguments during the visits about which group a particular tale or mythical character belonged to. Those of us children who had both Asian and African ancestors made it easy by saying that the spirits were half-Asian and half-African.

We always bragged that our own country and stories were the best, even though the stories were often the same or nearly the same. My favorite character in these shared stories was Papa Bois (his Trinidad name) or No-Mere-mang (as he was called in Surinam). In both countries he could appear in all sorts of different forms. Papa Bois could help or punish those lost in the forest, or help unhappy children. . .

ATLANTIC OCEAN

LEEWARD ISLANDS

CARIBBEAN SEA

WINDWARD ISLANDS

TOBAGO TRINIDAD

SURINAM

Papa Bois

Tara was unhappy and sulking; she did not want to go with her cousin Lennet and parents driving up and down Mount Aripo to see the scenery. Tara wanted to be with her friends in San Fernando. She and her friends were selected to help build the Tadjan for the Hosay parade.

Besides, Tara couldn't stand her cousin's bragging any longer. According to her, everything in Surinam was better than in Trinidad and Tobago. The Hosay Tadjan in Surinam was apparently the best in the world; far better than the one in Trinidad. Even the picnic that Tara's mother prepared was not as good as that of Surinam.

"In Surinam," said the cousin, "roti does not have peas in it. The thing with peas in it is dall pori, not roti." Tara turned to look through the window while her cousin continued. "In Surinam, our cars don't break down, we don't get stuck on mountains in broken cars. In Surinam . . ."

"In Trinidad we have snakes, lots of them, huge ones and tiny ones." Tara interrupted her cousin's bragging. "The very tiny snakes are worse. Those tiny snakes get through very tiny spaces." Tara pointed to the tiny opening by the car window. "One bite and you're gone!" Tara enjoyed the look of fright on her cousin Lennet's face. "We have no snakes in Surinam. The mongooses ate them all," replied Lennet nervously.

"Here we do. That's why my dad said to keep the window of the car closed while they went to get help." It had been raining, and the cars the two families were in could not get back up the steep hill. The hill had become slippery like marble and the cars kept sliding backward. The adults had gone down the hill to get help.

"I'm not scared," said Lennet, but she crawled into the corner of the back seat of the car anyway.

"Oh, and we have bush spirits. Did I tell you about them? The worst one is Papa Bois. He's got a long white beard that reaches nearly to his knees and his face is white, like chalk. When he grins, his teeth are half black and half white. And for feet he has hooves."

"I don't believe you," said Lennet, but she moved farther into the corner.

"Well, we did run over a wild animal, and Papa Bois protects animals."

"It was an accident," said Lennet, now petrified.

"Oh, yeah? Tell that to Papa Bois," said Tara.

Just then there came a
sharp and loud scream from where
Lennet had been cowering in the corner of
the back seat. "Th. . . There. . ." Lennet stammered,
pointing to the back window. There was a figure coming
toward them through the mist, and it was not one of the
fathers who had gone down to get help. It was a white-faced
man with a long beard and long, matted dreadlocks. His head
was covered and his long gray hair was wet. The strange figure
got nearer the car and tapped on the window, but Lennet
didn't hear. Lennet had fainted!

"You men, them coming with four-wheel truck, yes?
Them know the way now," said the figure and
smiled, showing a row of gold teeth. Then he
disappeared into the mist.

Tara just smiled.

Glossary

Anansy A spiderman who appears in West African and Caribbean stories.

Ancestors The people from whom we are descended—even those so far back in time that we do not know them by name.

Anjisa A special headdress worn by Surinam Kreoro women.

Bre A title before a person's name, meaning fellow or brother. Joel Chandler Harris wrote about southern Brer Rabbit stories.

Greo A name from Africa meaning a storyteller.

Hollanders People born in Holland, used in that country's old colonies in the Caribbean. Holland is formally known as The Netherlands.

Hosay A festival celebrating the story of two Hindu gods who were brothers. All people join in Hosay, not just Hindus.

Kreoro Surinam people who are of African descent.

Panji A wrap that goes around the body, said to originate in West Africa. Like many words, customs, and styles of clothing, they were brought to the Caribbean by African people who arrived in the region on slave ships.

Rite of passage A coming-of-age ceremony in which a boy or girl passes from childhood to adulthood.

Surinamers People born in Surinam.

Tadjan Brilliantly decorated towers built as part of the Hosay celebrations.

Books

Information books

Anthony, Suzanne. *West Indies* (Major World Nations). New York: Chelsea House, 1998.

Brownlie, Alison. *Jamaica* (Country Insights). Austin, TX: Raintree Steck-Vaughn, 1998.

Haverstock, Nathan. *Dominican Republic in Pictures* (Visual Geography). Minneapolis, MN: Lerner Publications, 1997.

Hintz, Martin. *Haiti* (Enchantment of the World, Second Series). Danbury, CT: Children's Press, 1998.

Hodge, Alison. *The West Indies* (Country Fact Files). Austin, TX: Raintree Steck-Vaughn, 1998.

Fiction and poetry

There are too many great Caribbean poets to list all their books, but you could look for John Agard, Benjamin Zephaniah, Grace Nicholls and Linton Kwesi Johnson on the bookshelves for starters. Derek Walcott, recent winner of the Nobel Prize for Literature, is from the Caribbean.

One of the most famous Caribbean novelists is V.S. Naipaul, who comes from Trinidad: his books *Miguel Street* and *The Mystic Masseur* tell about what it was like growing up in the Caribbean in the 1950s.

Web sites

www.camanews.com is a regular news site based in Barbados that offers a Caribbean-wide service on everything from sports to economics.

Caribbean Activities

Music is a big part of Caribbean life, and lots of different types are popular. Calypso, reggae, soka, salsa, and rap are among the types of music people listen to. You could get hold of a tape or CD of calypso music, then try to make up your own lines to the songs, but be warned: calypso can be pretty rude!

❢

Linton Kwesi Johnson, the poet and musician, sets his poems to reggae music. You could write a poem based on one of the stories in this book, then try setting it to music.

❢

Make up a dance performance based on **Anana, the Maker**. The main dancers could be Sun and Moon, with supporting dancers acting out the other parts, such as the Moon Jaguar.

❢

Imagine some of the characters in **The Flying Slaves**: the slaves who hear that they will be able to fly home if they don't eat salt, other people who don't believe the story, the children listening and then making their own plan to stop their parents from leaving them, and the tragic end of the story. You could make a play from this dramatic tale.

❢

Sunny-Limp Walks Again is set in an old school that was once a plantation house, but ghostly events don't have to take place in old buildings. Can you write a convincing ghost story set somewhere else? Don't forget to describe the setting, the thoughts that go through the characters heads' and how these thoughts make them act, as well as what they say and do.